DISASTER!

DISASTER!

Illustrated by Richard Bonson
Written by Richard Platt

DK PUBLISHING, INC.

A DK PUBLISHING BOOK

Senior Art Editor Dorian Spencer Davies
Senior Editor John C. Miles
U. S. Editor Camela Decaire
Managing Editor Sarah Phillips
Senior Managing Art Editor Peter Bailey
DTP Designer Karen Nettelfield
Production Charlotte Traill
Picture Research Joanne Beardwell
Mariana Sonnenberg

First American Edition, 1997
2 4 6 8 10 9 7 5 3 1

Published in the United States by DK Publishing, Inc.
95 Madison Avenue, New York, New York 10016

Copyright © 1997 Dorling Kindersley Limited, London
Text copyright © 1997 Richard Platt

Visit us on the World Wide Web at
http://www.dk.com

A catalog record is available
from the Library of Congress.

ISBN 0-7894-2034-1

Reproduced by Dot Gradations Ltd., Essex
Printed and bound in Italy by A. Mondadori Editore, Verona

CONTENTS

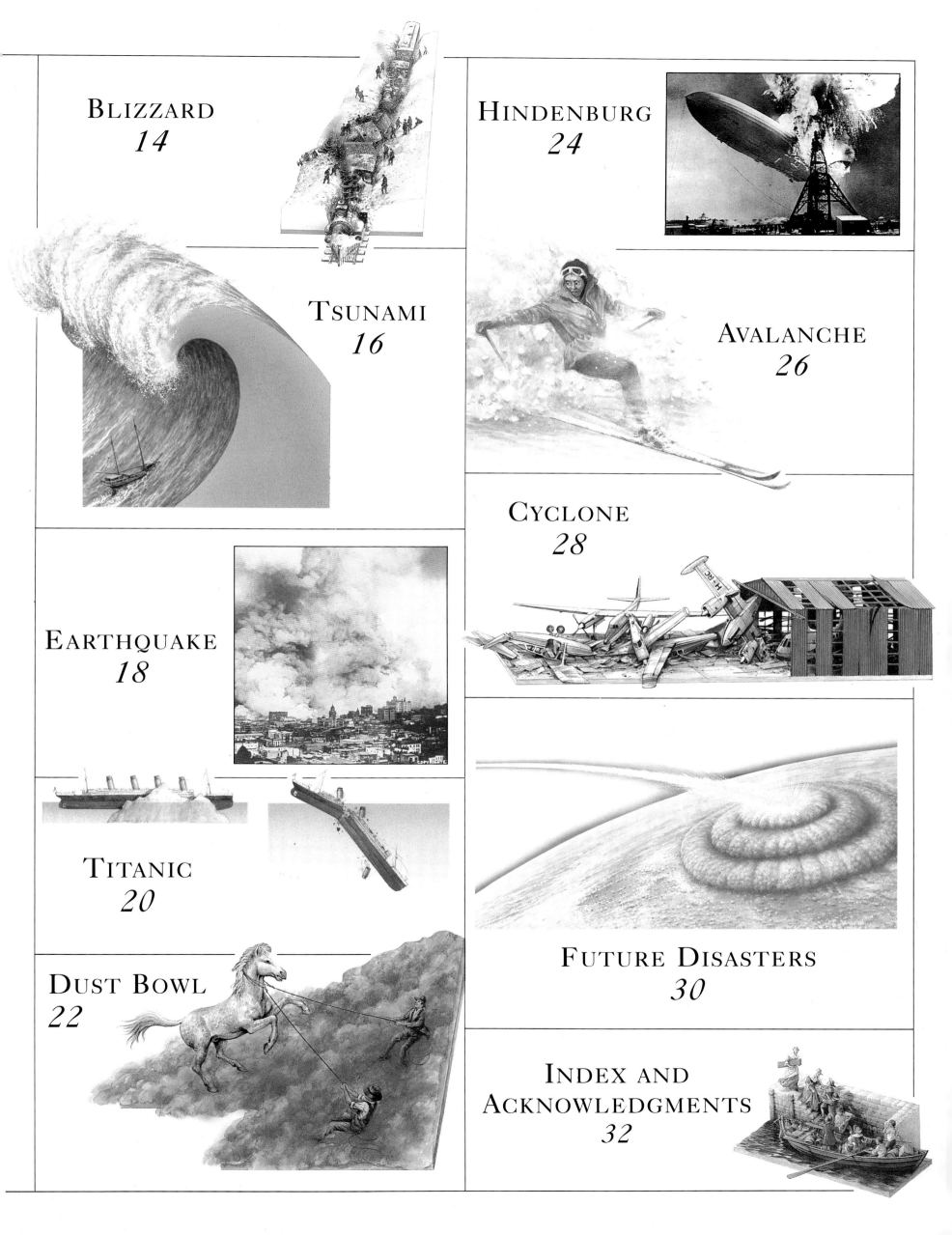

VESUVIUS

"SURELY IT COULDN'T BE VESUVIUS?" the people of Pompeii asked each other when the earth began to shake on August 24, AD 79. The volcano loomed over their southern Italian town, but they had no reason to fear it. The volcano had been quiet for so many years that no one could remember when it last erupted. Vesuvius soon answered the question on everyone's lips. With a deafening boom, it exploded. A day later, Pompeii was a tomb of mud and dust.

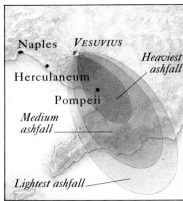

Deadly breeze
A northwest wind blew ash over Pompeii, burying the city.

Pompeii today
Cleared of ash, Pompeii now attracts thousands of visitors, and millions live in the surrounding area. A new eruption of Vesuvius could kill 500 times as many people as the eruption in AD 79.

Pompeii was a large, wealthy town.

Shaky start
AUG 24
The first tremors probably did not alarm the people of Pompeii. Earthquakes are common in the region and rarely do serious damage. But nobody could ignore the mountain when the eruption began. The summit of Vesuvius exploded. Lightning bolts lit up the vast cloud of ash and glowing cinders that shot high into the air.

On any normal day, crowds would have thronged in Pompeii's streets and lined up at the bakeries and stand-up café counters.

Earth tremors produced by the eruption shattered buildings in the town.

The explosion blew the summit off Vesuvius, and the rock and ash quickly fell to earth.

Luxury
Pompeii's most luxurious houses had attractive dining rooms and gardens. Beautiful mosaics covered the floors, and murals brightened the walls. The ash preserved all these details.

The earthquake struck as Pompeiians were breakfasting.

The cloud descends
AUG 25
While the ash cloud blotted out the sun, turning day to night, almost all of Pompeii's people fled. As a few lingered to gather belongings, ash and pumice flakes blanketed the ground. Overcome by the dust and fumes, they died in their homes surrounded by the precious objects they were trying to rescue.

Quick death
The ash cloud that fell on Pompeii rapidly entombed the town. Archaeologists found 2,000 bodies in its streets and buildings. The mudflow that engulfed nearby Herculaneum was slower, and all but 30 people escaped.

Rich and poor died side by side.

The story of a tragedy

1. Gas, dissolved in the magma (hot, liquid rock) beneath the volcano, blasted the eruption high in the air. Enough rock flew up to build 1,100 Great Pyramids.

The ash cloud also contained cinders and whole rocks.

Pressure built up in the magma chamber beneath the volcano due to movements in the Earth's crust.

Rocks as big as tennis balls fell near Vesuvius.

2. The explosion dispersed the magma, which solidified into a fine ash and began to fall to the ground.

3. The wind blew the ash cloud over Pompeii, engulfing the town. Nearby Herculaneum escaped, until rain turned the ash into mud, which flowed down the mountain to bury it.

Once the eruption had released the pressure of the magma, Vesuvius was quiet once more.

Lightning cloud
Steam and friction between airborne dust particles can charge the air around an eruption with static electricity. This causes spectacular lightning bolts.

Astonished survivors of the eruption saw that it had blown away the entire top of the mountain.

The volcano's cone was made up of many layers of ash, dust, and rock.

Pressurized gas within the vent forced the contents upward at twice the speed of sound.

The volcanic vent had been blocked with solidified magma.

Because so many people and things were entombed by the ash, Pompeii is the most complete record of Roman life to have survived.

Cast of thousands
As the bodies rotted away, they left perfect molds in the ash. By poring plaster into these molds, archaeologist Giuseppe Fiorelli (1823–1896) was able to re-create people's dying moments down to the tiniest detail. The plaster casts record even facial expressions and the textures of fabrics.

The ash protected the entombed people from the weather and vandals.

Distance and depth

The cloud was so dense that even 60 miles (100 km) away, ash fell 4 in (10 cm) deep.

The huge chamber filled with magma extended for 6 miles (10 km) beneath the volcano. Pompeii lay roughly the same distance southeast of Vesuvius. The town was so close that the ash blocked out all sunlight; the volcano's roar would have been deafening.

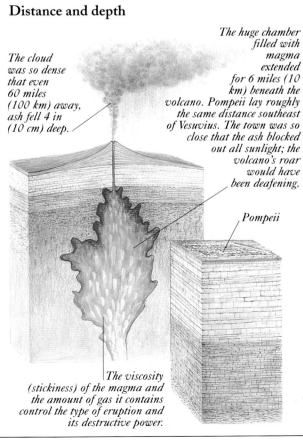

Pompeii

The viscosity (stickiness) of the magma and the amount of gas it contains control the type of eruption and its destructive power.

Fleeing citizens tied cushions or towels to their heads for protection.

Many people trapped in their homes tried unsuccessfully to use cloth to filter the choking dust from the air.

Bodies entombed by ash

Volcanic ash preserved the wall paintings.

Many dining rooms have been preserved at Pompeii.

AUG 26 Ash covers Pompeii
Ash fell for two days, crushing roofs and filling rooms. Heavy rain made the ash solidify like cement. Soon the town was covered to a depth of 19–23 ft (6–7 m). Survivors of the catastrophe abandoned Pompeii. The people of the region forgot its location. They even forgot its name, just calling the lost town "the City."

BLACK DEATH

DISASTERS DON'T ALL BEGIN WITH THUNDERBOLTS, explosions, or earth tremors. The greatest catastrophe in the history of the world was a silent, invisible killer – the plague. In the mid-14th century rats spread this disease throughout Europe. People called it the Black Death, or sometimes bubonic plague, because of the huge black buboes (swellings) that appeared on victims' bodies. The plague struck people already weakened by cold and hunger, and most of those who caught it died within a week. When the epidemic ended, it had killed a quarter of Europe's population.

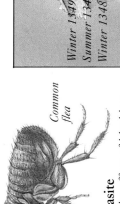

Common flea

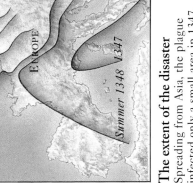

Winter 1349
Summer 1349
Winter 1348

Summer 1348   V347

EUROPE

1350

Deadly parasite
Plague had the effect of blocking rat fleas' guts. The fleas, unable to swallow the blood they suck, vomited it back on their victims, depositing the deadly bacterium.

Where it started
The 1347 outbreak probably began in the Black Sea port of Caffa. The town was under siege and the attacking Mongol army was catapulting plague-infected corpses over the walls. Ships returning to Italy then brought plague-carrying rats with them.

The extent of the disaster
Spreading from Asia, the plague infected only a small area in 1347. But by 1351, it had reached all of Europe except Poland.

Rats!
Mainly a disease affecting rats, plague is spread by fleas, which bite their rat hosts. When large numbers of rats die from plague, their fleas need new hosts, and begin biting humans.

The stone manor house belonging to the local lord was the grandest house in the village.

Most poor people worked on the land.

Bad living conditions made things worse. Most houses were tiny, cold, and damp, and families lived in one room.

The symptoms of plague were easy to recognize, and wealthy people fled from outbreaks.

People bitten by rat fleas developed bubonic plague, which produced a painful swelling in their groin or armpit. Sufferers later developed a cough, which spread the more infectious pneumonic (lung) plague. Its victims spat blood and turned blue.

Summer

1348

Even before the plague arrived, the English people were suffering. For the previous two years, cold, wet weather had ruined the crops, so food was scarce. A good harvest would have provided just enough for everyone, but the crops failed again, so people were weak and hungry. In August, infected rats arrived by ship at a southern coastal port, and travelers spread the disease from there.

Poor people could not flee: they had no transportation, and in any case, many of them were not allowed to leave without their lord's permission.

Rats lived in the thatched roofs, and among the straw and garbage on the floors.

"Where go you, stranger?"
Travelers brought news of the plague, but it soon became clear that the visitors themselves carried the infection. Soon villagers became suspicious of any stranger, and some hamlets posted guards to keep out everyone except local people.

While there were few deaths, plague victims received a decent burial.

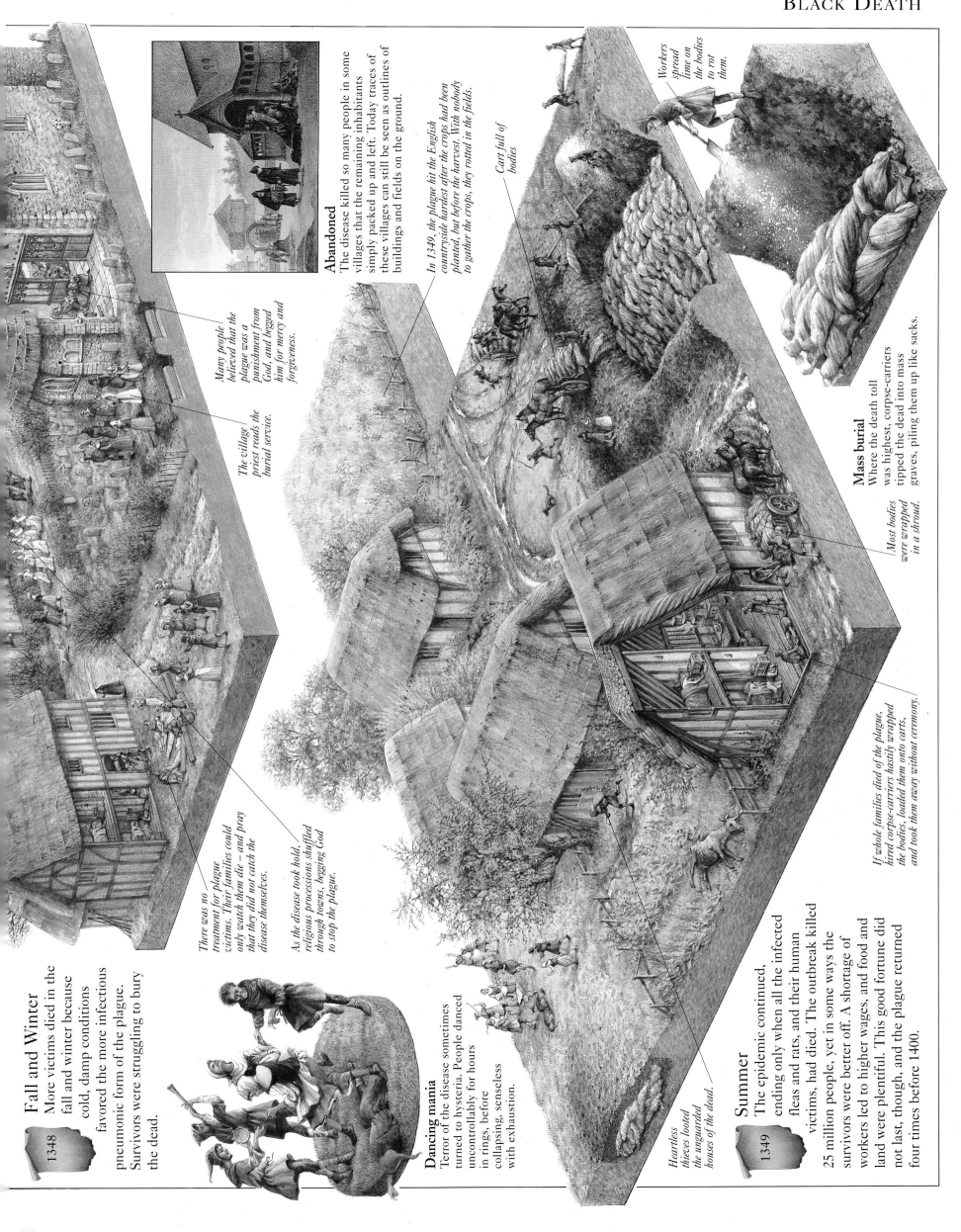

Fall and Winter

1348

More victims died in the fall and winter because cold, damp conditions favored the more infectious pneumonic form of the plague. Survivors were struggling to bury the dead.

Many people believed that the plague was a punishment from God, and begged him for mercy and forgiveness.

The village priest reads the burial service.

There was no treatment for plague victims. Their families could only watch them die – and pray that they did not catch the disease themselves.

As the disease took hold, religious processions shuffled through towns, begging God to stop the plague.

Abandoned

The disease killed so many people in some villages that the remaining inhabitants simply packed up and left. Today traces of these villages can still be seen as outlines of buildings and fields on the ground.

In 1349, the plague hit the English countryside hardest after the crops had been planted, but before the harvest. With nobody to gather the crops, they rotted in the fields.

Cart full of bodies

Workers spread lime on the bodies to rot them.

Mass burial

Where the death toll was highest, corpse-carriers tipped the dead into mass graves, piling them up like sacks.

Most bodies were wrapped in a shroud.

If whole families died of the plague, hired corpse-carriers hastily wrapped the bodies, loaded them onto carts, and took them away without ceremony.

Dancing mania

Terror of the disease sometimes turned to hysteria. People danced uncontrollably for hours in rings, before collapsing, senseless with exhaustion.

Heartless thieves looted the unguarded houses of the dead.

Summer

1349

The epidemic continued, ending only when all the infected fleas and rats, and their human victims, had died. The outbreak killed 25 million people, yet in some ways the survivors were better off. A shortage of workers led to higher wages, and food and land were plentiful. This good fortune did not last, though, and the plague returned four times before 1400.

THE GREAT FIRE

IN 17TH-CENTURY LONDON, FIRES WERE COMMON. So when Farrinor's bakery caught alight early on Sunday morning September 2, 1666, few people were alarmed. "Pish!" exclaimed the Lord Mayor when he was summoned, " . . . a woman could piss it out!" But the summer had been hot with very little rain, and the timber-framed buildings were as dry as dust. A strong wind fanned the flames and sparks leaped the narrow streets, setting fire to crowded houses and stores. By Tuesday, three-quarters of the old city was reduced to smoking ashes.

Wind and fire
Strong winds whip up flames and help fires spread. This Australian bush fire clearly shows the result.

The glow above London's night sky could be seen from 40 miles (64 km) away.

Burning fragments and sparks from Farrinor's bakery soon set nearby houses on fire. When one house caught fire, the whole street burned.

London houses had timber frames.

Houses were packed closely together.

London Bridge had houses and stores built on it.

Some people saved musical instruments, like this early keyboard.

Riverside wall

SEPT 2 2:00 am Sunday: Bakery burning
The fire started in a bakery in Pudding Lane, just north of London Bridge. Smoke and flames woke the baker and his family. They escaped across the roofs of neighbors' houses.

Mouth of oven

Base of oven

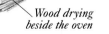
Wood drying beside the oven

The oven
In the 17th century, bakers heaped wood into their ovens, burned it, then raked out the ash before starting again. Most of them dried their fuel for the following day inside, or next to, the warm oven overnight. Even the tiniest spark could have ignited the drying wood.

The longer the fire burned, the more money the greedy watermen charged to save people and property.

SEPT 2 Sunday: Spreading flames
As the flames spread toward the river, people took to the water, carrying only their lightest and most valuable possessions. Many people buried gold and silver items to protect them. The fire set light to the wooden warehouses and wharves that lined the riverbanks. Many stored wine, brandy, lamp oil, resin, and tar, which exploded and burned fiercely.

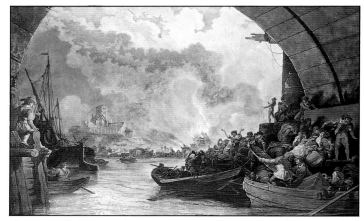

An artist's impression
This colored aquatint by J.C. Stadler, showing St. Paul's Cathedral ablaze, was taken from a 1799 painting by Philip J. Loutherbourg.

SEPT 3 — Monday: Demolishing houses

Firefighters attempted to stop the blaze by pulling down the houses in its path. However, citizens were reluctant to demolish their homes until they were actually ablaze.

As wooden steeples burned, bells crashed down and lead roofs melted.

The fire destroyed 84 of the city's 109 churches. Many, including St. Paul's Cathedral, were rebuilt by Sir Christopher Wren.

Sailors from the dockyards blew up houses with gunpowder.

Brick chimneys were left standing on their own after houses were destroyed.

Barrels of oil exploded like bombs.

To pull buildings down, firemen used long poles with hooks on the end, which they pulled with ropes and chains. These were called firehooks.

A human chain passed leather buckets of water up a ladder.

A firefighter fills a hand squirt from a tub. These squirts gave very little water pressure, so they were almost useless.

Pump on wheels

SEPT 4 — Tuesday: The wind dies

The navy fought the fire by blowing up houses with gunpowder. The explosions created gaps that the fire could not cross. But it was a change in the weather that really killed the fire: on Tuesday night the wind dropped, and the flames finally died.

Blaming foreigners

Rumors spread that foreign enemies had started the fire. Violent mobs roamed the streets attacking foreigners and Catholics. A Frenchman confessed to starting the blaze, and was hanged for the crime – though he was probably mentally ill and innocent.

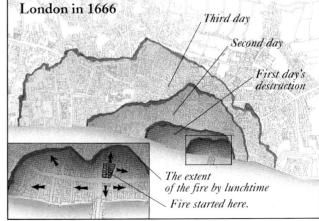

A vicar who saw an attack wrote, "a blacksmith . . . meeting an innocent Frenchman . . . felled him instantly to the ground."

London in 1666

Third day

Second day

First day's destruction

The extent of the fire by lunchtime

Fire started here.

Fire-mark

Fire insurance

As a result of the fire, Dr. Nicholas Barebone (c.1640–1698) started the world's first fire insurance company. An annual fee bought householders the protection of a private fire brigade, and compensation if their house burned down. A metal plaque called a fire-mark identified protected buildings.

Fighting fire

People attacked the flames with handheld squirts, which looked like large syringes. These were hardly more effective than water pistols, and the pump hoses could not reach roofs. Longer hoses were introduced from Holland a few years after the Great Fire.

The ashes of London

The fire burned 395 acres (165 hectares). Although only six people died, more than 100,000 were left homeless. Architects, including Sir Christopher Wren (1632–1723), planned a new city, but members of the government could not agree on the "best" plan, leaving the rebuilt area a disorganized muddle.

HUANG HE FLOOD

WHEN TORRENTIAL RAIN ENDED A LONG DROUGHT in the summer of 1935, the farmers of the North China Plain celebrated. But rain brought danger, too. It swelled the great Huang He (Yellow River), which flowed between dikes (embankments) high above the fields. Every year the water rose higher than the year before – sometimes as much as 35 ft (10 m) above the surrounding plain. In mid July the banks burst and the river flooded 6,000 sq miles (15,000 sq km): an area half the size of Belgium. The floods drowned thousands of people, and hundreds of thousands more died in the famine that followed. But tragically, the 1935 floods were not unusual: throughout China's history the river has burst its banks two years in every three, earning the Huang He the nickname "China's Sorrow."

Changeable waterway
The Huang He (Yellow River) meanders across the North China Plain. After flooding, its receding waters have often established a different course. Since 2278 BC, the river has changed course at least 15 times. In 1935, the floods covered the shaded area.

Destroyed villages
Stone was scarce in the Huang He valley, and fired bricks costly, so these were reserved for temples and the houses of wealthy people. Ordinary families built their homes from sun-dried mud bricks, and gave them thatched roofs. Both these materials crumbled in the rising waters.

Besides kaoliang, farmers grew cotton, soya, wheat, corn, garlic, sweet potatoes, cucumbers, and radishes.

One of the most important crops was kaoliang, a plant a little like sugarcane. It has edible seeds that are used to make wine.

The water was very shallow, so only special flat-bottomed boats, called junks, could travel down it.

In places the dikes were so wide that roads were built on the top.

In some areas, 20 inches (half a meter) of rain fell in two days. This made the river burst its dikes.

Some junks were big enough to haul stone and large quantities of grain.

The fertile soil of the flood plain

JUNE **Reinforcing the dikes**
The people strengthened the banks of the Huang He in 1935, as they did every year. Their main building materials were the stalk and root of the kaoliang plant, bound into bundles. Willow trees stabilized the banks and supplied reinforcing stakes. Blocks of stone protected banks on the bends, where the water did the most damage.

JULY **Waiting**
When rain began, flood watchers were posted along the top of the dikes. Constant repairs were made to small breaks, but by mid July, the water lapped at the top of long sections of the walls.

Terrified villagers ran for their lives.

How the river level rose

The yellow mud that gives the Yellow River its name causes the flooding. When water flows slowly, the mud that is swept along with it settles. Eventually, this mud raises the riverbed – and therefore the level of the water – which spills over.

Dike

Rising riverbed and water level

1. The river flows normally between the dikes.

2. Mud deposited on the bed of the river raises the water level.

3. Eventually the river overflows the dikes, flooding the nearby lowlands.

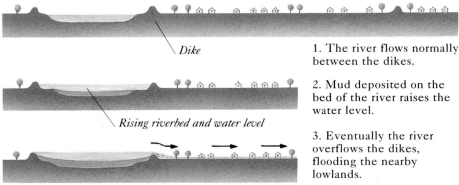

Productive land
The Huang He deposits deep, fertile mud each time its banks burst. So, despite the destruction caused by the floods, the farmers need the floods to enrich the land.

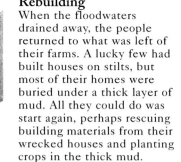

Rebuilding
When the floodwaters drained away, the people returned to what was left of their farms. A lucky few had built houses on stilts, but most of their homes were buried under a thick layer of mud. All they could do was start again, perhaps rescuing building materials from their wrecked houses and planting crops in the thick mud.

Houses were buried under a thick layer of mud.

Farmers plowing their fields sometimes broke through the roofs of buried houses.

Hemp ropes

Counting the cost
There is no accurate count of the total number killed by the 1935 floods since, as this contemporary image illustrates, the Huang He flows through many heavily populated areas. When it burst its banks in 1887, 900,000 people may have died. Only a few drowned; most starved when mud covered their crops.

Repairing the gap
To repair the gap in a broken dike, workers first made sausage-shaped bundles of rocks and kaoliang stalks. Hemp ropes held the 50-ft (15-m) bundles together. The dike builders then suspended a net of hemp ropes above the gap, and filled it with earth and the bundles of kaoliang stalks and rocks, before lowering the net to stop the flow.

Bundles of rocks and kaoliang stalks

The rushing floodwater swelled to six times the volume of Niagara Falls.

The entire river flowed out through more than 1,000 breaks in the dikes, leaving a dry riverbed downstream.

Many refugees fled in small boats called sampans, which had oars at the stern (back) end. Some sampan owners collected floating valuables instead of rescuing people.

Those who managed to climb to safety braved terrible conditions until they were rescued. Many helped save others.

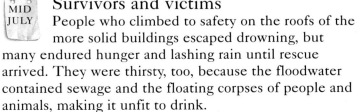

Decaying bodies polluted the water and helped cause epidemics of bubonic plague, cholera, and dysentery.

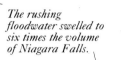

The dikes break
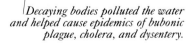 When the water reached the brim, villagers worked feverishly to raise the dikes. But the river also scoured out the banks below the surface, and in places the dikes gave way without warning. As the water rushed out, it widened the gaps, until breaches nearly 1 mile (1.6 km) across opened up in some places.

30,000 people whose homes had been destroyed could not return until the following March.

Survivors and victims
People who climbed to safety on the roofs of the more solid buildings escaped drowning, but many endured hunger and lashing rain until rescue arrived. They were thirsty, too, because the floodwater contained sewage and the floating corpses of people and animals, making it unfit to drink.

BLIZZARD

THE FORECAST SAID THE WEATHER IN NEW YORK would be "fair and colder" on Monday, March 12, 1888. No wonder the people of New York blinked in amazement when they awoke on Monday morning. A fantastic blizzard had brought their city to a standstill. Gale-force winds blocked streets with drifting snow. Ice snapped telegraph wires. The snow caused food shortages and 400 people froze to death. Life only returned to normal after a week. More than a century later, New Yorkers still shiver when they talk of the disastrous blizzard of '88.

Frozen buildings
A crust of ice broke gas and water pipes that entered buildings from outside. After the blizzard, developers hurried to protect these vital services by burying them underground. City engineers also planned an underground subway that snow could not stop.

20 inches (half a meter) of snow fell, but the wind drove it into deep drifts. In some places it even reached second stories.

Horse-drawn transportation was the best way to stagger through the snow. But the horses' manes and tails quickly became thick with ice.

The wind blinded those who faced it, froze their ears, and numbed their hands. They felt as if their breath was rammed down their throats.

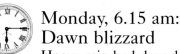

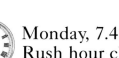

Four died when a New York and Harlem train tried to crash through a snowdrift.

People had to shout to be heard over the storm.

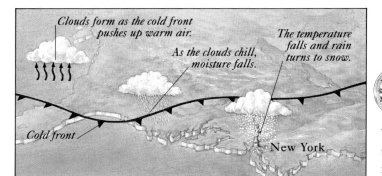

Clouds form as the cold front pushes up warm air.

As the clouds chill, moisture falls.

The temperature falls and rain turns to snow.

Cold front

New York

Birth of a blizzard
The cause of the blizzard of '88 was a mass of cold air moving east. This cold front forced warm, moist air upward, resulting in snow. A low air pressure system then followed, creating strong winds. The combination of wind and snow produced the blizzard.

Monday, 6.15 am: Dawn blizzard
Heavy rain had drenched New York on Sunday. A little after midnight, the rain turned to snow. Strong winds ripped down signs and telegraph wires already heavy with ice. By dawn, thick snow carpeted the streets. As more fell, horses struggled to pull cabs. Streetcars came off their tracks. A few brave New Yorkers struggled out to work.

Monday, 7.42 am: Rush hour chaos
The storm worsened, making rail travel chaotic. Ice disabled the telegraphs used by signal men to communicate between stations, and snow covered the tracks. Many trains came to a standstill, blocked by snowdrifts.

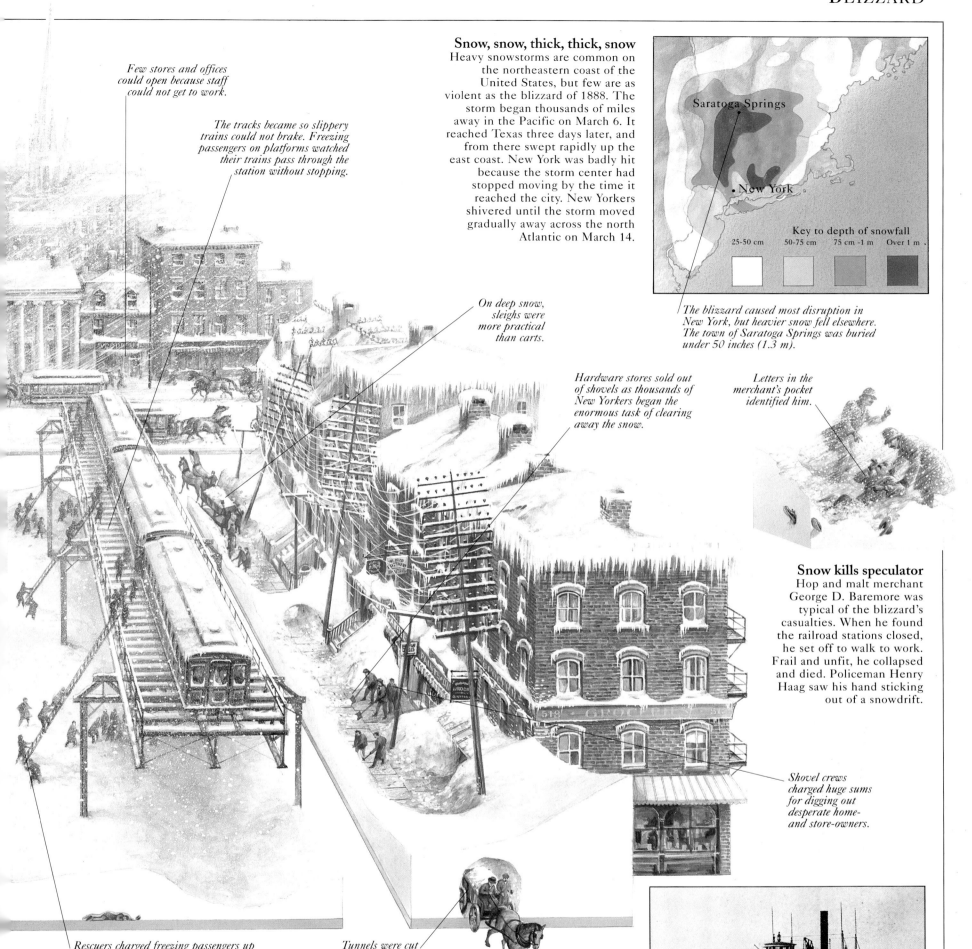

Few stores and offices could not open because staff could not get to work.

The tracks became so slippery trains could not brake. Freezing passengers on platforms watched their trains pass through the station without stopping.

Snow, snow, thick, thick, snow
Heavy snowstorms are common on the northeastern coast of the United States, but few are as violent as the blizzard of 1888. The storm began thousands of miles away in the Pacific on March 6. It reached Texas three days later, and from there swept rapidly up the east coast. New York was badly hit because the storm center had stopped moving by the time it reached the city. New Yorkers shivered until the storm moved gradually away across the north Atlantic on March 14.

Key to depth of snowfall

| 25-50 cm | 50-75 cm | 75 cm -1 m | Over 1 m |

The blizzard caused most disruption in New York, but heavier snow fell elsewhere. The town of Saratoga Springs was buried under 50 inches (1.3 m).

On deep snow, sleighs were more practical than carts.

Hardware stores sold out of shovels as thousands of New Yorkers began the enormous task of clearing away the snow.

Letters in the merchant's pocket identified him.

Snow kills speculator
Hop and malt merchant George D. Baremore was typical of the blizzard's casualties. When he found the railroad stations closed, he set off to walk to work. Frail and unfit, he collapsed and died. Policeman Henry Haag saw his hand sticking out of a snowdrift.

Shovel crews charged huge sums for digging out desperate home- and store-owners.

Rescuers charged freezing passengers up to $2 – the cost of a meal in a railroad dining car – to step down.

Tunnels were cut through the biggest snowdrifts.

Monday, noon: Trapped in trains
The elevated trains that managed to leave their depots ground to a halt, leaving 15,000 travelers stranded high above the ground in unheated cars. Enterprising people in the streets below brought ladders to rescue them – for a price. Some passengers on mainline trains were stranded for two days without food or heat.

Tuesday, 10.00 am: Digging out
Snow stopped falling on Tuesday. New York was still cut off from the outside world, though, because the storm had brought down telegraph and telephone links. Shovels, bread, milk, and coal were scarce. Life returned to normal only slowly. As people shoveled the snow, they uncovered the storm's victims, frozen solid. More bodies appeared when huge snow banks melted weeks later.

Ice traps the ferries
The storm sank ships all along the eastern coast of the United States. The sea froze as the cold weather continued, and the rising tide forced ice floes into New York Bay. The ice halted ferry traffic, and as many as 10,000 people walked over the East River from Brooklyn to Manhattan.

TSUNAMI

THE GIANT WAVE ROLLED toward the northeastern coast of Japan at dusk on June 15, 1896. Those who saw it tried to raise the alarm. They shouted "Tsunami! Tsunami!" – Japanese for the huge waves caused by earthquakes. Few heard, for the wave made a louder sound, like distant cannon fire. By the time it reached the shore, the tsunami was a black wall of water 80 ft (24 m) high. Minutes later, when the waters had drained away, all that remained of bustling fishing villages was mud and splintered wood. The tsunami had destroyed everything.

Waves as big as buildings
At worst, tsunamis can engulf the biggest buildings when they crash ashore, as this painting shows. Many have less dramatic effects; they raise the sea level like an unusually high tide. Where the tsunami of 1896 entered a bay or inlet, the wave took all the wreckage and deposited it inland. Where the coastline was open, it swept everything out to sea.

The crest of the wave glowed with the phosphorescence produced by algae and sea creatures.

10,000 fishing boats disappeared.

The tsunami roared into an area of fishing communities.

The wave carried many people out to sea.

Even the largest ships could not escape the wave.

Wreckage and rocks carried by the wave added to the destruction.

JAPAN

HONSHU ISLAND

Miyako

Kamaishi

Kesennuma

Ishinomaki

The force of the tsunami

Where the wave struck
The tsunami came ashore on the northeastern coast of Honshu, the biggest of Japan's four main islands. Japan is in one of the world's most geologically active areas. Three earthquakes shake the country each day, but few produce a tsunami as destructive as that of 1896.

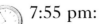 **7:55 pm: The wave approaches**
There had been 13 minor earth tremors on June 15. Everyone in the small fishing villages ignored them, perhaps because there had not been a bad tsunami for 40 years. In the distance, the approaching wave looked like a shadow. Rumbling toward the shore, it towered over buildings, its crest glowing white.

8:00 pm: The tsunami strikes
Those who saw or heard the huge wave approaching hurried upstairs for safety, but the tsunami smashed their homes. In many villages, only one or two people in every ten escaped – often those who had rushed to high ground. In all, 27,000 people were killed, and the wave tore apart 175 miles (280 km) of Honshu's coastline.

The cause of a tsunami

Vibrations and shocks in the earth's crust cause tsunamis. Earthquakes, landslides, and volcanic eruptions can all trigger the waves. At sea, the wave may be only waist high. Shallow water slows the wave down, greatly increasing its height.

The tsunami crosses the ocean as fast as a jet plane.

An undersea earthquake creates a wave.

The shape of the shore affects the destructive power of the wave.

The sequence of events

1. Just before the 1896 tsunami struck, the sea level suddenly fell, as if there was a very low tide. In some places, the water drew back 600 yards (550 m).

2. Where the wave hit a low coastline, it engulfed the shore in deep water for about five minutes. The flooding lasted longer in estuaries and long, narrow inlets.

3. When the wave ebbed, it sucked away not only the debris of destroyed houses and ships, but also parts of the land itself, changing the shape of the coastline.

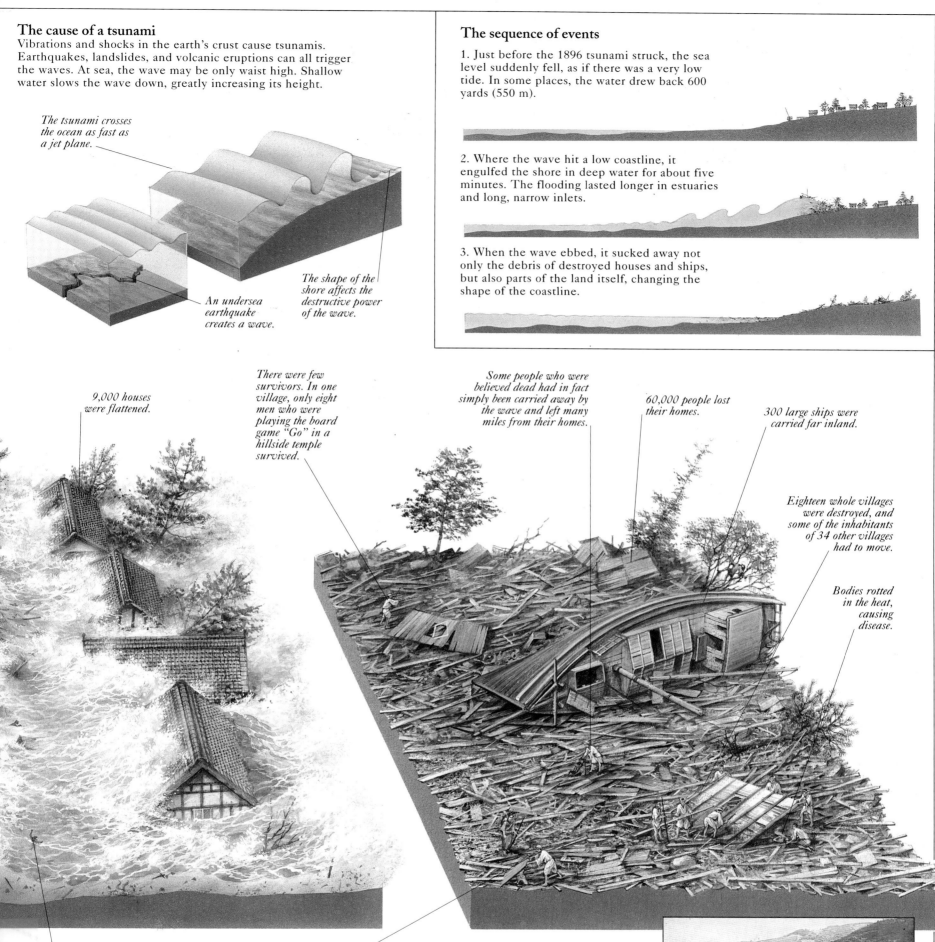

9,000 houses were flattened.

There were few survivors. In one village, only eight men who were playing the board game "Go" in a hillside temple survived.

Some people who were believed dead had in fact simply been carried away by the wave and left many miles from their homes.

60,000 people lost their homes.

300 large ships were carried far inland.

Eighteen whole villages were destroyed, and some of the inhabitants of 34 other villages had to move.

Bodies rotted in the heat, causing disease.

Even strong swimmers were helpless.

So many drowned that there were not enough survivors to bury them.

🕗 **8:25 pm:**
Searching the wreckage
Survivors searched for relatives, but without food, clothes, or medicine, they could do little to help the injured. News of the disaster spread slowly: the tsunami had cut telegraph links, and mountains kept the affected area isolated from the rest of the country. By the time help arrived, disease or hunger had killed some of those who had escaped drowning.

Japanese homes
Traditional Japanese houses are not made of paper, as many assume, but of timber and plaster. Their frames bend to absorb the shock of an earthquake, but a tsunami smashes them to splinters.

Devastated villages
Photographers and journalists from Tokyo newspapers traveled with relief workers to the scene of the catastrophe. Their reports and pictures show the debris and wrecked ships where fishing communities once thrived.

EARTHQUAKE

HALF A MILLION PEOPLE SHARED THE SAME nightmare on Wednesday, April 18, 1906. To a roar like that of 100 express trains, their beds rocked and their houses collapsed. The people of San Francisco woke to discover an earthquake wrecking their city. Earthquakes are violent tremors that occur when the plates of the earth's crust slide past each other. These sudden movements of the earth's surface create huge ocean waves and the ground rips open, shaking buildings apart. This earthquake was destructive enough, but worse was to come. Sparks flew as electric cables snapped and gas pipes broke. In minutes, wooden buildings were on fire. The blaze raged for three days. When it died, it left the city a charred ruin.

San Andreas Fault
The boundary where the Pacific and North American plates meet under San Francisco is called the San Andreas Fault. It stretches roughly 600 miles (1,000 km) from just north of the city to the Gulf of California.

Town of tinder
The discovery of gold in California caused the population of San Francisco to grow rapidly. In 1846, three years before the Gold Rush, fewer than 500 people lived there. By 1906, the city had grown a thousand times. But nine out of ten buildings were hastily constructed wooden structures.

The shock set all the church bells ringing amid the crashing of falling buildings.

Wednesday, 5:00 am: The city slumbers
In 1906, San Francisco was a booming city. But at 5:00 am, the business district was silent and almost deserted. The rising sun would not catch the taller steel and stone buildings for another hour. In the poorer areas, a few laborers were setting off to work from their cheaply built wooden shanties.

San Andreas fault

Tectonic plates
Beneath our feet, the earth seems solid. But, actually, the earth's crust (hard outer shell) is split into sections called tectonic plates, which are in constant, slow motion. The boundaries of these plates are shown in red on the map on the left. The plates float on the earth's mantle – a layer of hot, partly melted rock. Where they meet, the plates slide against each other, causing earthquakes.

Wednesday, 5:13 am: Earthquake!
A survivor described the moment when the earthquake struck: "The whole street was undulating. It was as if the waves of the ocean were coming toward me." The earth shook for about three minutes, then a lesser aftershock quickly followed. The quake fractured streets and sent masonry crashing down, but destroyed only a few buildings. It left many more unsafe, or leaning precariously at crazy angles.

Focus and epicenter

Most earthquakes happen in the lithosphere – a zone that extends some 60 miles (100 km) down from the earth's surface. The source of vibrations within the lithosphere is called the focus. The epicenter of the earthquake is the point on the earth's surface directly above the focus.

Epicenter

Lithosphere

Shock waves can travel right through the earth.

Shock waves

Focus

Earthquake waves

Earthquake tremors travel in waves moving at 2.5 miles (4 km) a second. The waves spread out from the focus, bending and reflecting where the earth's composition changes.

Strong winds fanned the flames, which consumed much of the central area over three days.

Rebuilding the city

San Francisco's tragedy brought worldwide sympathy, and relief aid flooded the city. Work to repair damaged buildings began almost immediately. Demolition teams pulled down dangerous structures and pushed the charred wreckage into the sea. Then construction workers began rebuilding. Twenty thousand houses went up in the three years after the quake.

Soldiers acted as riot police. However, some got drunk on looted alcohol and shot at survivors.

The quake buckled the rails of San Francisco's famous streetcar system and put 250 miles (400 km) of railroad track out of action.

Saturday, 7:45 pm: A city in ashes

By Friday evening, only one fire on the waterfront was still burning. Fireboats fought bravely to save the docks. At times, they had to turn the hoses on their decks as embers falling from the sky started fires. But by Saturday morning, the fires were under control. In total, 850 people had died and 28,000 buildings were destroyed or damaged. The army housed 300,000 homeless people in tent cities and fed them from soup kitchens. Elsewhere, troops shot looters. But within three years, a new city was to rise from the ashes.

Wednesday, 9:00 am: The fire rages

Gas leaked from pipes that burst in the quake. Nearly 50 fires started in the downtown area within 15 minutes of the quake, and by early morning there was a powerful blaze. The earthquake broke water pipes and put the city's fire-alarm system out of action. Desperate fire-fighters even pumped sewage onto the burning buildings. Later, troops tried to create fire-breaks by blowing up whole streets, using explosives and artillery shells.

City in flames

Bad planning and bad fire control spread the flames that burnt the city. San Francisco had many cisterns (water storage tanks) beneath the streets. However, these had run dry because the city would not pay to maintain them. The fire-fighters did not know the correct way to dynamite the buildings. They tried to create gaps too wide for the fire to cross. Instead, their explosions often exposed more timber to the flames.

TITANIC

A VAST FLOATING PALACE SLID through the icy Atlantic Ocean. It was April 14, 1912, and the world's biggest passenger ship, the *Titanic*, was on its first voyage. As the ship steamed along, more than 300 wealthy people dozed in rooms on the upper decks. Below, three times as many people slept in cheaper quarters. All felt safe, for they believed the *Titanic* was unsinkable. They were wrong. Just after midnight, the ship hit an iceberg and sank. More than 1,500 people drowned or died of exposure in the freezing water.

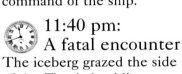

Avoiding the icebergs
The *Titanic*'s Captain knew of the ice hazard, so he steered south, hoping to sail through warmer water, which would melt any ice.

11:30 pm: Danger ahead
The *Titanic* had been sailing for three days before reaching ice-filled waters. At 11:40 pm, a lookout in the crow's nest (lookout post) spotted a huge iceberg. He rang a warning bell and bellowed "Iceberg, right ahead!" into the telephone to alert the First Officer, who was in command of the ship.

11:40 pm: A fatal encounter
The iceberg grazed the side of the *Titanic*, buckling the steel plates that formed the hull of the ship. This allowed water to pour in. The First Officer closed the watertight doors, but the gash was too long – the *Titanic* was doomed.

Many of the third-class cabins were in the bow, which sank first.

Frozen islands
Icebergs are vast floating islands of ice – the biggest are the size of Belgium. Some tower several hundred feet above the sea, yet only one-eighth of any iceberg floats above the water. The iceberg that sank the *Titanic* had broken off the end of a glacier in Greenland.

The "unsinkable" *Titanic*
Steel walls divided the *Titanic*'s hull into 16 compartments. Closing the interconnecting doors sealed each compartment, and the ship was designed to stay afloat even with four sections flooded. This is why people thought the ship could not sink.

The Fourth Officer fired distress rockets every five minutes.

On the bridge, the First Officer was in command.

The lookout who spotted the iceberg was in the crow's nest.

First-class cabins

Many lifeboats were lowered before they were full.

The iceberg gashed six of the Titanic*'s compartments (shown in blue).*

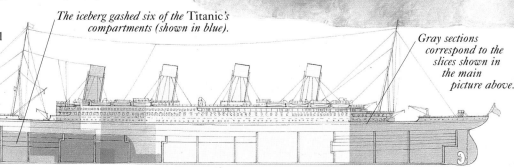

Gray sections correspond to the slices shown in the main picture above.

12:45 am, April 15: To the lifeboats!
Around midnight crew members began to prepare the lifeboats, and at 12:45 am the first boat rowed away. Many people could not believe the ship was sinking and refused to board the lifeboats.

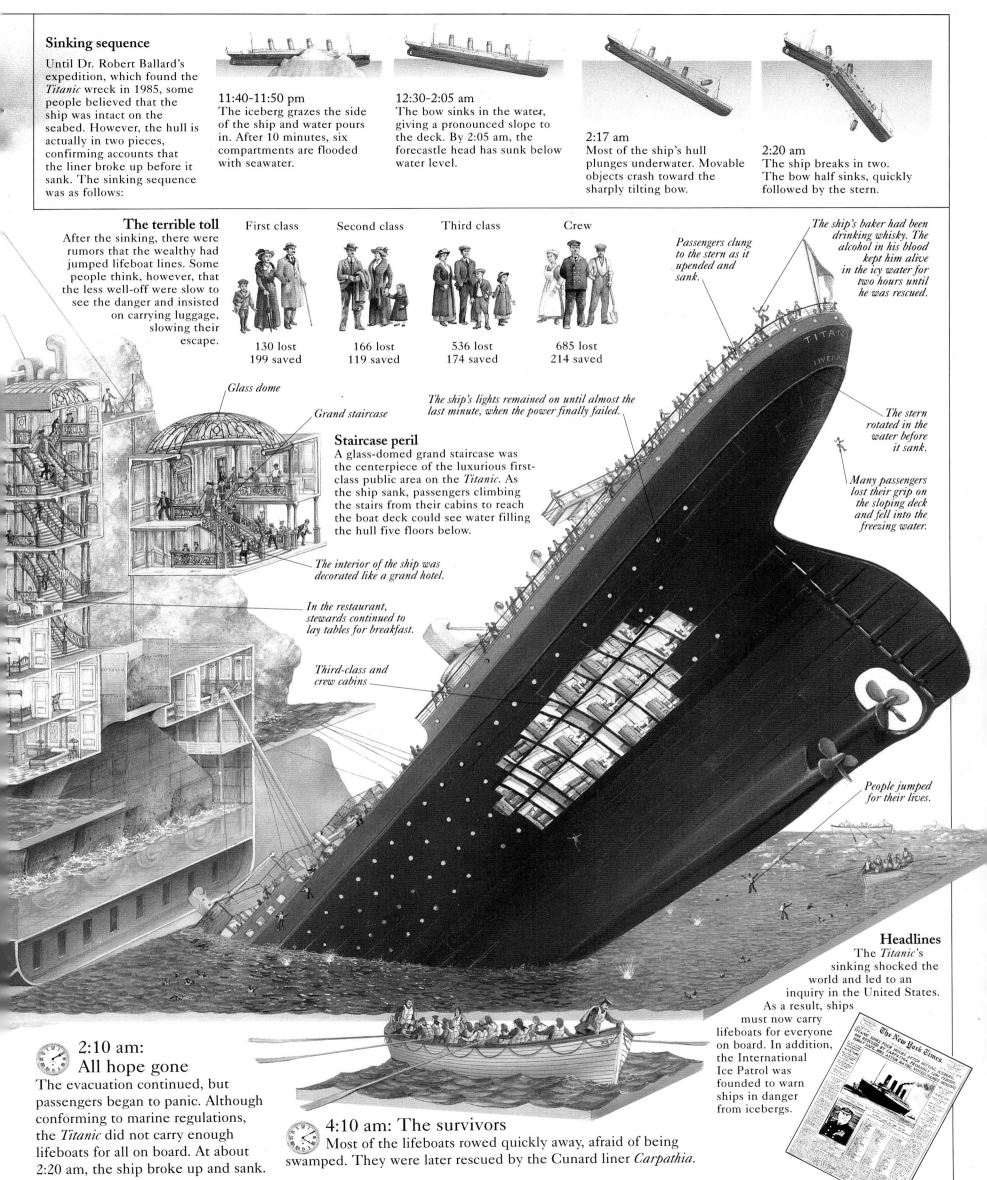

Sinking sequence
Until Dr. Robert Ballard's expedition, which found the *Titanic* wreck in 1985, some people believed that the ship was intact on the seabed. However, the hull is actually in two pieces, confirming accounts that the liner broke up before it sank. The sinking sequence was as follows:

11:40-11:50 pm
The iceberg grazes the side of the ship and water pours in. After 10 minutes, six compartments are flooded with seawater.

12:30-2:05 am
The bow sinks in the water, giving a pronounced slope to the deck. By 2:05 am, the forecastle head has sunk below water level.

2:17 am
Most of the ship's hull plunges underwater. Movable objects crash toward the sharply tilting bow.

2:20 am
The ship breaks in two. The bow half sinks, quickly followed by the stern.

The terrible toll
After the sinking, there were rumors that the wealthy had jumped lifeboat lines. Some people think, however, that the less well-off were slow to see the danger and insisted on carrying luggage, slowing their escape.

First class	Second class	Third class	Crew
130 lost 199 saved	166 lost 119 saved	536 lost 174 saved	685 lost 214 saved

The ship's baker had been drinking whisky. The alcohol in his blood kept him alive in the icy water for two hours until he was rescued.

Passengers clung to the stern as it upended and sank.

The stern rotated in the water before it sank.

Many passengers lost their grip on the sloping deck and fell into the freezing water.

Glass dome

Grand staircase

The ship's lights remained on until almost the last minute, when the power finally failed.

Staircase peril
A glass-domed grand staircase was the centerpiece of the luxurious first-class public area on the *Titanic*. As the ship sank, passengers climbing the stairs from their cabins to reach the boat deck could see water filling the hull five floors below.

The interior of the ship was decorated like a grand hotel.

In the restaurant, stewards continued to lay tables for breakfast.

Third-class and crew cabins

People jumped for their lives.

2:10 am: All hope gone
The evacuation continued, but passengers began to panic. Although conforming to marine regulations, the *Titanic* did not carry enough lifeboats for all on board. At about 2:20 am, the ship broke up and sank.

4:10 am: The survivors
Most of the lifeboats rowed quickly away, afraid of being swamped. They were later rescued by the Cunard liner *Carpathia*.

Headlines
The *Titanic*'s sinking shocked the world and led to an inquiry in the United States. As a result, ships must now carry lifeboats for everyone on board. In addition, the International Ice Patrol was founded to warn ships in danger from icebergs.

Dust Bowl

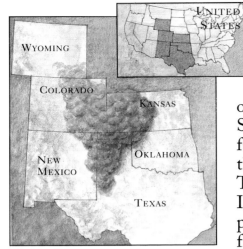

Dust bowl states
The terrible drought of the 1930s hit the whole of the Great Plains region: a huge, dry plateau that was once grassland.

Lawrence Svobida looked out at his Kansas farm. Five years earlier it had been a mass of waving, golden wheat. But in 1936, the wheat had gone. So, too, had the fields themselves. Drought and bad farming had turned the soil to dust, and winds then blew the dust away. Nothing grew on the land stripped of soil. The wind drove the fine dust everywhere in black blizzards. It filled tractor engines. It stopped watches. It clogged people's lungs. Like thousands of others, Lawrence Svobida finally gave up farming in 1939. In the previous eight years, he had harvested only one wheat crop. The barren land he left behind came to be called the Dust Bowl.

Storm clouds
From afar, the dust storms looked simply like black, low clouds. But as the storm struck, the clouds engulfed everything on the ground and in the air.

At first, cattle grazed on the unfenced "range."

Wind pumps raised water from deep wells, so cattle did not need access to a river to drink.

Large fields
Farmers like Lawrence needed tractors and combine harvesters because fields were huge. A typical farm had 800 acres (325 hectares) – the area of 450 soccer fields.

Even though doors and windows were tightly closed, by the time a storm had passed everything inside the house would be covered in a blanket of dust. The dust got everywhere, even inside cupboards.

Sowing the seeds of disaster

1931 Early settlers had found the Great Plains like deserts. Rainfall was unpredictable, but by the 1870s, after a run of unusually wet years, farmers began to raise cattle. Soon, easily available barbed wire meant the cattle was penned in instead of being left to roam. But in dry years, there was not enough grass. On land that could support ten cattle, farmers grazed 17. The cattle ate every scrap of grass and eroded the soil. So, too, did plowing. Between 1900 and 1910, wheat farming increased six fold. Together, the cattle and the plow removed the natural plants that held the soil in place.

Rounding up the animals
When the black blizzards approached, farm hands struggled to move terrified animals to safety. Those left out of doors became ill and often died. The dust killed wild animals, too. It buried rabbits; small birds could not fly in the dirt laden wind and dropped exhausted to the ground.

The drought begins

1932 The previous four years had produced good harvests, but in 1932 the drought set in. February gales snapped off the young wheat shoots, then lifted the dry soil. In the east of the Great Plains, there was more than two feet (60 cm) of fertile soil. Farther west, soil was less than a third as deep. The winds soon exposed a "hard pan" of calcium carbonate in which nothing grew.

What caused the dust?

Many of the worst-affected farmers worked small plots of land, which they overgrazed, turning pasture to near-desert. The government had encouraged them to plow the land for wheat, a practise that made matters worse. Plowing loosened and powdered the soil, which the wind then blew away.

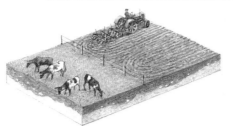

1. Only the topsoil – the thin surface layer – was fertile enough for farming.

2. Overgrazing and stubble-burning removed the plants that held the topsoil together.

3. Strong winds easily blew away the dry, loosened topsoil, leaving earth in which nothing would grow.

During a dust storm it became so dark, people needed lights indoors all day.

In strong winds, clouds of valuable soil traveled as far as the east coast, and dust was even found on ships 300 miles (480 km) off the coast.

In many areas the soil was a distinctive colour – red, black, or yellow – so people could tell where a dust cloud had come from.

Dust piled up against buildings like snowdrifts and farmers had to dig themselves out.

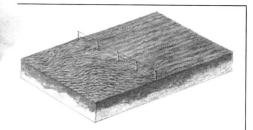

Empty homesteads
When farmers abandoned their wooden shacks and moved out, neighbors who had stayed on took over the vacant land.

Dust ruined tractors, making them worthless.

Suffocation killed many thousands of cattle. Many more died from eating dust as they desperately foraged for what little grass remained.

Farmers who had once owned huge estates abandoned them to look for work as mere laborers.

Californians nicknamed migrants "Okies" because so many of them came from the state of Oklahoma.

Families packed everything they owned into hand carts or battered cars.

Killer dust engulfs the plains

1936 Many farmers had enough savings to ride out a couple of bad years, but the drought continued. To try to keep out the dust, farmers hung wet cloth over their doors and windows, but in a "blow," everyone ate, drank, and breathed dust. Lung disease rose dramatically. Families who stayed fit were often ruined financially, and when they could not repay loans, the banks went bust. By 1936, it was clear that an environmental and human catastrophe had hit the region.

Abandoning the land

1937 The United States government began handing out aid to a million farming families as early as 1933. Farmers also received advice on how to stop soil erosion. But for many, this was not enough. Half a million people abandoned their land and headed for California. Those who stayed on did best. They bought land at rock-bottom prices and planted trees as wind-breaks. When the drought ended in 1938, they harvested bumper crops.

No hope farmers
To try to get help for the Dust Bowl farmers from the U.S. government, photographs were taken to show the terrible conditions they lived in.

HINDENBURG

IN 1936, THE ULTRAMODERN WAY to cross the Atlantic was aboard the German airship *Hindenburg*. As big as a skyscraper, this ship floated freely above the ground thanks to hydrogen-filled cells (giant bags). Hydrogen is 13 times lighter than air, but it also burns fiercely – during a routine landing on May 6, 1937, leaking hydrogen caught fire, reducing the airship to a blazing wreck in under 30 seconds.

Big bang
The *Hindenburg* blazes at Lakehurst, New Jersey. A newsreel film of the disaster was shown in movie theaters worldwide.

The rudder steered the airship to port (left) and starboard (right).

St. Elmo's Fire

A ball of flame about 10 ft (3 m) wide burst through the outer cover. One onlooker said that the first flames were like "a mushroom-shaped flower bursting into bloom."

The tailplane pointed the airship up or down.

The airship's rigid metal frame gave it a cigar shape, which reduced friction with the air.

One of four diesel engines that powered the airship

Death of a giant

1. The *Hindenburg* was floating near the mooring mast when flames first appeared.

2. As the fire spread, the airship became tail-heavy.

3. Flames shot forward to the airship's nose as the tail fell.

4. All 16 gas cells had burned by the time the airship hit the ground.

6:25:00 pm: First flames

Just before the fire began, the *Hindenburg*'s tail end lost lift, and the outer fabric began to flutter, indicating a possible gas leak. Releasing ballast failed to level the ship, so six crew members went forward to weigh down the nose section. At 6:25 pm, fire started in the fifth gas cell.

6:25:15 pm: Fire spreads

When the fire spread to the other cells, the gas they contained exploded, shaking the airship's frame. Passengers and crew could see the flames licking down the sides of the fabric cover. Some jumped for their lives.

Passenger accommodations

Tickets were expensive – the price of two automobiles – so passengers expected luxury accommodations. Public and private rooms were on two decks, recessed in the belly of the airship.

The windows opened – even at 3,600 ft (1,000 m).

Passenger cabin

Stairway

Lounge

The bathrooms had showers, but the spray was feeble and a timer limited water use.

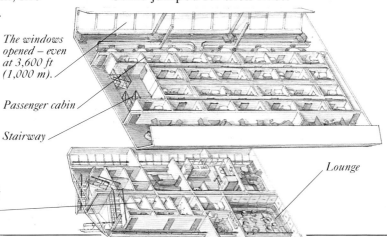

6:25:30 pm: Impact!

Within half a minute, all the cells had burned. Without hydrogen gas to lift it, the ship's weight increased from nothing to 245 tons (222 tonnes), and it crashed to the ground, a heap of tangled metal.

Center-section gas cells

As the hydrogen gas blazed, the fabric covering incinerated like paper.

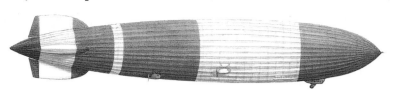

Key to main picture

The orange sections correspond to the slices shown in the main picture below.

St. Elmo's fire

The atmosphere's natural electric field may have ignited the *Hindenburg*. The floating airship had the same electrical charge as the surrounding air. The mooring ropes that secured the airship allowed electricity to flow from the atmosphere to the airship, setting the leaking gas ablaze. The electrical discharge may have been St. Elmo's fire, a flickering bluish glow. Sailors in the 1600s noticed St. Elmo's fire surrounding the tops of masts during storms.

Filling gas cells with helium (which does not burn) would have prevented the disaster. However, helium was not widely available in Germany in the 1930s.

Three crew members in the bow escaped by clinging on until the wreck hit the ground.

On the ground

The fire killed 36 people – a third of those on board. Investigators combed the wreckage for clues, but could only guess at the cause of the accident. Regular transatlantic flights did not start again until 1945 – and airplanes were used instead of airships.

Control cabin

Bursting ballast tanks on the burning wreck doused a 14-year-old mess boy with water, saving his life.

Eight of the nine crew members in the control cabin escaped. Some jumped, others ran from the wreckage.

AVALANCHE

SNOW FELL THROUGHOUT the night in the Swiss village of Andermatt, and it continued all morning. Just before 2 pm, the eastern end of the village was engulfed by an avalanche. As the snowfall continued, drifts on the mountain above grew dangerously deep. If they grew deeper, the village was in danger of another avalanche, more destructive than the first. Controlled explosions could prevent this, so avalanche experts fetched a mortar – a tube that launches a small bomb high into the air. They took aim at the threatening snow, and fired. Not one, but two avalanches thundered down the mountain, crushing a house. But this was not the end of the avalanches. In the early evening, yet another avalanche crashed down. By nightfall on January 20, 1951, snow had killed ten people in Andermatt.

Andermatt and the Alps
The Alps are Europe's greatest mountain range. Andermatt is at the end of the St. Gotthard Pass, where the Alps are low enough for a road to link Italy and Switzerland.

GERMANY
FRANCE
SWITZERLAND
Andermatt
AUSTRIA
ITALY

Birth of an avalanche
When weather conditions make fallen snow unstable, the slightest shock can start an avalanche. Even the sound of church bells can start the snow moving.

Types of avalanches

1. Slab avalanches separate in large blocks when melted water separates a slab of snow from the rock underneath.

2. Airborne powder avalanches begin soon after fresh snow falls. The huge mass of snow compresses the air in front of it, creating a destructive shock wave.

3. Dry, loose snow often occurs after a heavy fall. It slides along the ground and usually comes to rest quickly, but can turn into a more dangerous airborne powder avalanche.

4. Wet snow avalanches are a hazard during spring. Snow becomes saturated with water, and moves slowly downhill.

🕐 **4:15 pm:** Mortar firing
The mortar team intended to set off a controlled avalanche that would not endanger the village. It fired a shell into the snow high up on the mountain.

🕐 **4:16 pm:** Avalanche!
Seconds after the mortar shell exploded, thousands of tons of powdery snow roared and hissed down the mountain, and could have buried the mortar team.

🕐 **4:20 pm:** Snow chaos
In fact, the shell produced two avalanches. These destroyed a house, and covered the village's main street to a depth of 15 ft (4.5 m). Fortunately, they caused no loss of life.

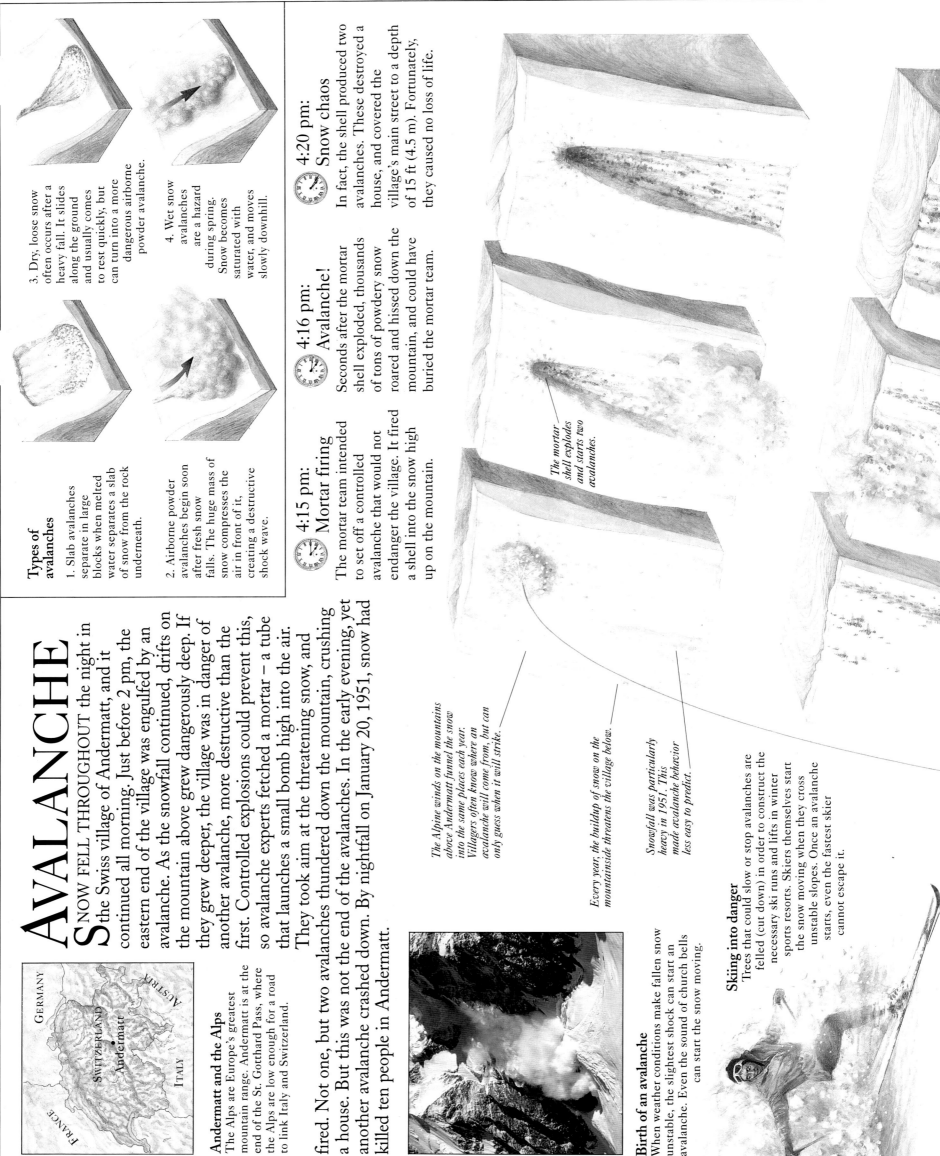

The Alpine winds on the mountains above Andermatt funnel the snow into the same places each year. Villagers often know where an avalanche will come from, but can only guess when it will strike.

Every year, the buildup of snow on the mountainside threatens the village below.

Snowfall was particularly heavy in 1951. This made avalanche behavior less easy to predict.

The mortar shell explodes and starts two avalanches.

Skiing into danger
Trees that could slow or stop avalanches are felled (cut down) in order to construct the necessary ski runs and lifts in winter sports resorts. Skiers themselves start the snow moving when they cross unstable slopes. Once an avalanche starts, even the fastest skier cannot escape it.

Rescuers at work

Locating buried survivors was slow – and depressing – work. Rescuers walked forward in a line, probing the snow with long sounding rods. They were more likely to find bodies than survivors: few people buried in snow live longer than half an hour. Those trapped in buildings are likely to survive for longer.

Dogs search much faster than people with sounding rods. Contrary to legend, dogs don't carry brandy barrels on their collars.

Force of destruction

An avalanche may carry hundreds of thousands of tons of snow at speeds three times faster than highway traffic. This gives the snow roughly half the power of the engines that lift the space shuttle into orbit. In Andermatt, the avalanches demolished sturdy buildings. Other avalanches have smashed whole areas of forest.

The tumbling snow covered the road and railroad line leading to the St. Gotthard Pass, and cut vital power lines in the village.

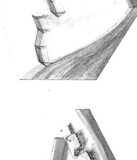

Track of mortar shell

Hazardous slopes

Centuries of farming have created treeless meadows from which snow slides easily. The people who live in these areas are in constant danger from avalanches.

Three hundred rescuers searched the tightly packed snow. During the afternoon, they found the bodies of a family. They continued searching for five other missing people.

Stopping the slide

Wedges of earth faced with stone can divide the avalanche so that it passes harmlessly on either side of a threatened village or building.

Explosives – usually shells fired from a mortar – can start small avalanches. This stops the snow from building up to unsafe depths.

Snow fences built high on the slope can also help stabilize the snow.

Forest trees are among the oldest and most effective ways of slowing avalanches.

CYCLONE

YOU CANNOT MOVE. You cannot see. You cannot speak. In a cyclone, all you can do is cling to something, and pray the wind and rain don't sweep you away. On Christmas Day 1974, one of these whirling tropical storms hit Darwin, the capital of Australia's Northern Territory. Nicknamed "Tracy," the cyclone formed over the ocean to the northwest, and grew in power as it moved toward the coast. When Tracy reached land, she caused terrible destruction. The people of Darwin took shelter for six terrifying hours; when they crept out, they found their town destroyed.

Crushed houses
"Imagine taking a matchbox … and crushing it with your foot." This was how one eyewitness described the damage that cyclone Tracy wreaked on Darwin's flimsy houses. Storm-proof homes have now replaced those destroyed in the 1974 cyclone.

The children of Darwin were looking forward to Christmas, unaware of what the day's events would bring.

🕘 **9.30 pm: Cyclone on the way!**
Cyclone warnings alerted Darwin's people to Tracy's approach on Christmas Eve. Many people ignored them since cyclones often threaten Australia's north coast, and there had been many false alarms. Cyclones usually came ashore in areas where few people lived. Preparations for Christmas continued. People even made up songs about cyclones never reaching Darwin.

Winds gusting to 185 mph (300 kph) threw people against walls and fences.

How big was it?
Hurricanes are like a huge, but thin, disk. Some are 380 miles (600 km) across. If Tracy was scaled down to be as wide as an LP record, the record would be a third of its normal thickness, and the eye one-seventh of the usual hole size.

Many people sheltered in windowless bathrooms, where they were safe from flying glass.

When the cyclone returned, people found themselves blown in the opposite direction.

🕛 **12.00 am: Tracy hits the city**
Around midnight, the cyclone reached Darwin. It tore through the flimsy houses, ripping off roofs. The storm picked up cars as if they were toys, tossing some into swimming pools. By 1:00 am, power lines snapped, cutting off electricity. There was great relief when the winds dropped suddenly three hours later.

🕓 **4.00 am: The eye**
Many people thought the storm was over, but they were wrong. The cyclone's "eye" – its calm center – was passing over. The winds returned, as hard as before, but now from the opposite direction. Anyone who had left shelter to return home was caught by the returning storm.

Tracy moves in

Cyclones are also called typhoons or hurricanes, depending on where they occur in the world. They start as small thunderstorms over warm oceans, which begin to swirl together. As the winds grow stronger, the cyclone spins across the ocean. But when it passes over land, the winds drop.

December 21
Satellite photographs showed a cyclone forming over the Arafura Sea.

December 22
Tracy approached Darwin. Forecasters hoped it would bypass the city.

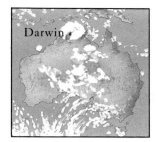

December 25
The cyclone engulfed Australia's northern tip, with its eye over Darwin.

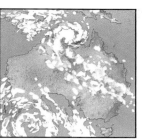

December 26
Tracy became less intense as it moved east across the Gulf of Carpentaria.

Destruction at the airport

At Darwin airport, the cyclone scattered small planes, damaged larger aircraft, and tore the roofs off hangars and terminals.

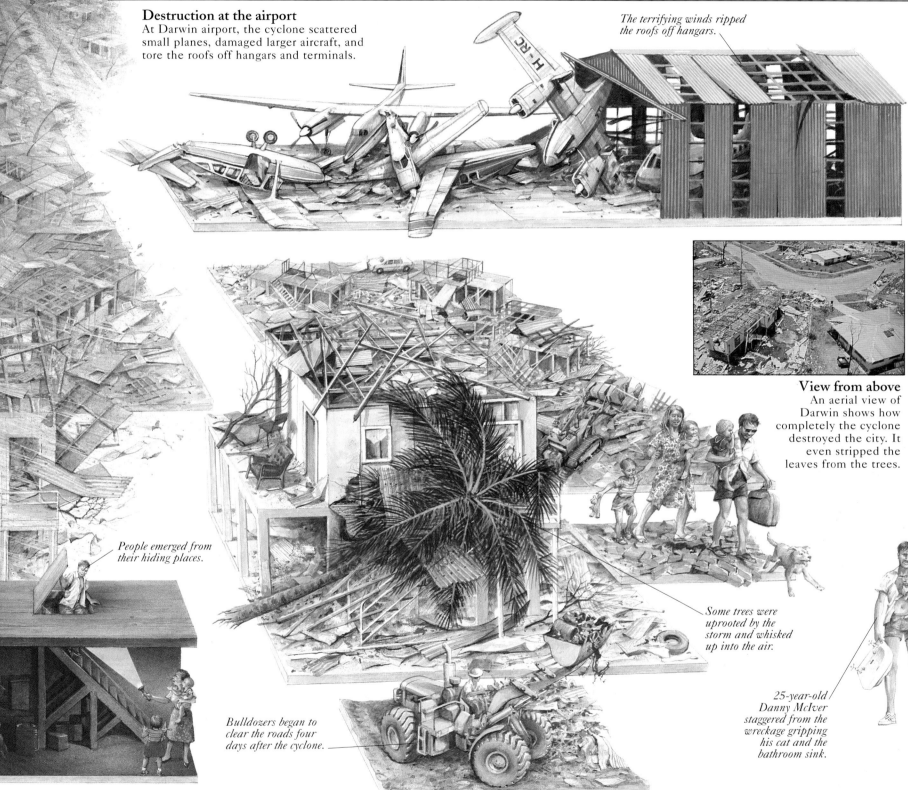

The terrifying winds ripped the roofs off hangars.

View from above
An aerial view of Darwin shows how completely the cyclone destroyed the city. It even stripped the leaves from the trees.

People emerged from their hiding places.

Some trees were uprooted by the storm and whisked up into the air.

Bulldozers began to clear the roads four days after the cyclone.

25-year-old Danny McIver staggered from the wreckage gripping his cat and the bathroom sink.

6.00 am: A city destroyed

Families crawled out from their wrecked homes soon after dawn. Tracy had destroyed nine in every ten homes. The cyclone had killed nearly 50 people, most of whom had suffocated. The rest of the city's 45,000 people had a lucky escape – when a cyclone had hit Bangladesh three years earlier, 300,000 people had died.

Noon: picking up the pieces

Darwin had no homes or power. The storm had also cut off water supplies, and for three days, people were unable to wash. Doctors and nurses worked to vaccinate the population against diseases that spread quickly in hot, dirty conditions. But by late evening, aircraft were already bringing in relief supplies. Many people escaped to safety by air. Some would not see their homes again for three years, but they would return to a new city, rebuilt with safer, stronger houses.

FUTURE DISASTERS

Could a disaster destroy life on earth? 65 million years ago, it nearly did. A meteorite the size of Mount Everest collided with our planet and its impact probably caused the extinction of the dinosaurs. If a meteorite just one-fifth as big struck the earth tomorrow, it would wipe out the human race. Such collisions happen only twice every million years, so the risk is small. But there would be nothing we could do to prevent it. Other kinds of catastrophes are more likely and easier to avoid. Rising carbon dioxide levels in the atmosphere are already affecting the earth's climate. If they continue, the polar ice caps may melt, swelling the seas and drowning coastal cities. Yet we could avoid this disaster by conserving rain forests and burning less coal, oil, and gas. Industry is poisoning our environment with nuclear or toxic waste and chemicals that destroy the earth's protective ozone layer. If a disaster ends human life on earth, it's likely to be an environmental disaster. The end will come not with a bang, but with a whimper.

Deforestation makes animals extinct because they cannot live in isolated pockets of forest.

Rain forest destruction

About four-tenths of the earth's land is covered by forests. But they are shrinking fast. Trees lock up carbon in their leaves and timber, and felling them releases it as carbon dioxide gas (CO_2). This deforestation puts as much CO_2 into the atmosphere each year as all the gas, coal, and oil burned in the United States. Rising CO_2 levels cause global warming, which may raise sea levels. Eventually, low-lying areas such as Bangladesh or the Netherlands could disappear under the waves. Global warming may also turn other regions into hot, dry deserts.

Green and brown rectangles have been cleared for farming.

Rain forest shows up emerald green in this satellite view of Brazil.

Logging the forest

Each decade, buzzing chain saws clear an area of tropical rain forest the size of Egypt. The loggers cut the trees for their valuable timber, or to clear land for farming.

Comet disaster

Circling around the sun, comets are like "dirty snowballs." They trail fluffy tails of glowing dust and vapor. Most pass harmlessly in space a long way from earth. But every century or so, a large comet passes between earth and the moon. In the next million years, one of these comets is likely to strike earth as a meteorite. Its impact would be six million times bigger than the atomic bomb that destroyed the Japanese city of Hiroshima in 1945. It would start a firestorm, releasing smoke and dust that would block out the sun. Plants could not grow, and animals and people would starve.

Meteorite crater

When asteroids (minor planets) collide in space, they break into rocky or metallic pieces. When they fall to earth, they are called meteorites. This crater in northeastern Arizona was caused by a meteor probably 25,000 years ago. It is 1,385 yd (1,265 m) across and deep enough to hold a 60-floor building.

Bio disaster

New diseases – and some familiar ones – threaten our world with bio-disaster. Antibiotic drugs that doctors have used successfully for 80 years no longer kill some common bacteria. Novel diseases, such as the Ebola virus, are spreading. Ebola victims (above) bleed to death horribly. There is no cure. Rapid transportation is also making older diseases more of a threat. In 1994, ice cream prepared in a single factory spread salmonella (food poisoning) all over the United States. It made 224,000 Americans sick.

Ozone disaster

High in the sky, a layer of ozone protects the earth from ultraviolet radiation (UV). But air pollution has thinned the ozone barrier, and in the 1980s a hole appeared in it above Antarctica. Unless there is international cooperation to limit the use of ozone-damaging chemicals, more UV will reach the earth, causing skin cancer, blindness, and crop damage.

This satellite picture shows the hole in the ozone layer.

Earthquake disaster

Natural hazards such as earthquakes and tsunamis don't get worse as time passes. However, as the earth's population grows, so, too, does the loss of life when these disasters strike. The population of the San Francisco area has tripled since the 1906 earthquake, and there is even a rail tunnel bored straight through the San Andreas fault. Sixty-one people died in a small quake that struck in 1994 (see above), but a repeat of the 1906 earthquake would kill many more.

The approaching comet is visible for a year or so before impact. Friction with the atmosphere turns the comet into a fiery ball.

Even a 33-foot (10-m) comet has several times the energy of the atomic bomb that destroyed the Japanese city of Hiroshima in 1945.

INDEX

ACKNOWLEDGMENTS
DK would like to thank the following
people for helping with this book:

Design: Joanne Earl, Ann Cannings,
Joanna Pocock
Editorial: Francesca Baines, Shirin Patel,
Nancy Jones, Robert Graham
Index: Chris Bernstein

Picture credits:
t=top; c=center; b=bottom; r=right; l=left.
Bridgeman Art Library: Guildhall Library,
Great Fire of London (1799), JC Stadler
20/21bl; **Corbis-Bettman:** 28/29br; **Frank
Lane Picture Agency:** 10cl, Australian
Information Service 15cr; **Getty Images:**
14tl, 24tr, 25cr, 25br, Keystone 11tl; **Ingrid
Morejohn:** 18br, 19tl; **Mary Evans Picture
Library:** 21tl, 29br; **N.A.S.A:** 14bl, 31cr;
Natural History Photographic Agency:
31cr; **Planet Earth Pictures:** David E.
Rowley 10tl; **Popperfoto:** 14/15tl, 31tr; **Rex
Features:** 31/32tc; **Robert Harding Picture
Library:** Tony Wattham 2tcl, Carol Jopp
29bl; **Science Photo Library:** David Hardy
28tl, 32bl,32cl; **Topham Picturepoint:** 26tl,
27br; **Zefa:** 3tc.